W9-ASC-734

Immigration
ISSUES

Refugees and Asylum

Jim Gallagher

ReferencePoint
Press®

San Diego, CA

LIBRARY OF CONGRESS CATALOGING-IN-PUBLICATION DATA

Names: Gallagher, Jim, 1969– author.
Title: Refugees and Asylum/by Jim Gallagher.
Description: San Diego, CA: ReferencePoint Press, 2020. | Series:
  Immigration Issues | Includes bibliographical references and index.
Identifiers: LCCN 2019043694 (print) | LCCN 2019043695 (ebook) | ISBN
  9781682827673 (library binding) | ISBN 9781682827680 (ebook)
Subjects: LCSH: Refugees—Juvenile literature. | Emigration and
  immigration—International cooperation—Juvenile literature. | United
  States—Emigration and immigration—Government policy—Juvenile
  literature.
Classification: LCC HV640 .G35 2020 (print) | LCC HV640 (ebook) | DDC
  325/.21—dc23
LC record available at https://lccn.loc.gov/2019043694
LC ebook record available at https://lccn.loc.gov/2019043695

Contents

Seeking a Safe Place

Wars are fought by soldiers, but they greatly disrupt the lives of civilians. Homes, schools, hospitals, businesses, roads, electrical infrastructure, and water and sanitation systems are often damaged or destroyed. Marketplaces that once bustled with activity are ruined, and businesses can no longer function. When national governments can no longer protect their citizens from violence, people must leave their homes to protect themselves and their families. Often, they may leave their country altogether and seek safety and shelter in another country. These victims of war and conflict are known as refugees.

Since 2011 the country of Syria has been torn apart by a civil war between the government and insurgent groups. Both sides have resorted to brutal tactics, with the Syrian government accused of using chemical weapons and barrel bombs in civilian neighborhoods. Since the Syrian civil war began, over 560,000 people have been killed, and about 12 million Syrian civilians have been forced to leave their homes. More than 5.1 million Syrians have fled the country altogether, becoming refugees. International organizations estimate that half of the Syrian refugees are children.

Fearing for Their Lives

One of these children, a sixteen-year-old girl named Walaa, describes frightening experiences that are typical of many refugees. "I was with my family at my home in Syria and we were preparing a dinner to have a nice meal together," she recalls.

> Suddenly the power goes off and darkness prevails. A moment later the sky lights up . . . from an explosion. Then all light is gone and all we can hear is screaming. Another explosion goes off and the screaming gets louder and louder. Death was around us, between us and we were waiting for our turn. My little brothers started to cry and I had to be strong for them, although I was afraid too.[1]

Walaa's family survived the night, but the civil war had come to their village. Fearing for their lives, Walaa and her family left their home and most of their belongings behind in 2015. They traveled to her grandmother's house in another town, where nine people lived together in a small room for a year and a half. However, as the fighting spread, even that modest shelter was not safe. Eventually, Walaa and her family left Syria altogether, traveling to neighboring Jordan.

Once they crossed the border into Jordan, Walaa and her family were considered refugees. Under international law, refugees are entitled to protection, or asylum, from neighboring countries. In some cases a refugee will be granted permission to live and work in the country until it is safe to return home. Refugees can also decide to settle permanently in another country that agrees to accept them. In Jordan, Walaa's family was able to live with other refugees in a temporary camp, where they could be safe and receive food, shelter, and medical care.

But life was not easy for Walaa's family, because her parents had trouble finding work or private housing that they could afford, and Walaa and other young refugee children were not permitted to attend Jordanian schools. "The Syrian children are not thinking about having fun or playing or making friends, they have bigger things to worry about," Walaa writes. "All they are thinking about is how to sleep not hungry, not thirsty or not cold. And if they actually will have a place to sleep tomorrow or will they be on the street as their parents can no longer afford the rent."[2]

Refugees and Migrants

Syria is far from being the only danger-ous place in the world. Due to ongoing conflicts today, large numbers of refugees are fleeing from conflict zones in places like Afghanistan, the Central African Republic, the Democratic Republic of the Congo, Myanmar, Somalia, Sudan, and South Sudan. Worldwide, the total number of refugees has grown steadily since 2010, resulting in the worst refugee crisis since the end of World War II. In 2019 the United Nations estimated that there were about 25.9 million refugees worldwide.

"The Syrian children are not thinking about having fun or playing or making friends, they have bigger things to worry about. All they are thinking about is how to sleep not hungry, not thirsty or not cold."[2]

—Walaa, a sixteen-year-old Syrian refugee

In news reports the terms *refugee*, *migrant*, and *asylum seeker* are often used interchangeably. However, these terms have specific and important meanings in national and interna-tional laws. A *migrant* is a person who leaves his or her country for any reason other than fleeing war or a campaign of persecu-tion by his or her government. Migrants may be trying to escape extreme poverty, seeking better job opportunities, or hoping to join relatives who have gone before them. According to a re-cent United Nations report, the number of international migrants worldwide has grown rapidly over the past decade, from 220 mil-lion in 2010 to 258 million by 2017.

Millions of migrants currently live in the United States, and hun-dreds of thousands of others are waiting for the opportunity to get into the country. Among them are Violetta Monterroso, who left Guatemala in November 2018 and traveled with her husband and three children to the US-Mexico border. They waited for months in a migrant camp in Tijuana, Mexico, for their turn to meet with US immigration officials to request asylum in the United States.

Asylum is a protection granted to foreigners who can prove that they meet the international legal definition of a refugee and have a "credible fear" of persecution or torture upon returning to their home country. Monterroso told authorities that her family left Guatemala because a group of thugs had threatened to kill their children if they did not pay the gang a monthly "protection fee" for their small business. "There is nobody that can protect us there," she said. "We have seen in the other cases, they kill the people and kill their children."[3]

Critical Legal Distinction

Although migrants like Monterroso often fear street gangs or drug cartels in their home countries, these threats do not entitle them to refugee status. A person is classified as a refugee only when that person's government cannot protect him or her from the effects of a war or civil war, as in Sudan and Syria, or actively persecutes that person due to his or her religion, gender, racial or ethnic group, or other characteristics. For example, in Myanmar, a minority ethnic group called the Rohingya has been subject to government-organized discrimination for decades. Since 2016 more than 650,000 Rohingya refugees have fled to neighboring Bangladesh to escape mass killings and the destruction of villages by Myanmar's military. In Monterroso's case, however, the Guatemalan government and its police forces are not the ones persecuting her family. Instead, her family is fleeing from gangs and drug cartels.

Without refugee status, most countries—including the United States—consider migrants like Monterroso and her family to be no different from other immigrants. They are subject to laws and policies that determine who can live and work within a country's borders. This means that countries can deport any migrant who enters the country without proper documentation or otherwise violates immigration laws.

In recent years hundreds of thousands of migrants have crossed the US border illegally, then surrendered to border patrol officers and requested asylum. A person who is granted asylum is entitled to the same sort of protections that a refugee receives. In fact, under international law the terms *asylum seeker* and *refugee* are synonymous. However, under US law, an asylum seeker (also called an asylee) is distinct from a refugee. One difference involves where the person is processed. A refugee is interviewed outside the United States before being accepted into the country. An asylee must already have reached US soil before making a request for asylum. Another difference is that there is no limit on the number of asylees who can be granted permission to live and work in the United States each year, while there is a limit, set annually by the president and Congress, on the number of refugee admissions.

Syrian refugees flee Syria on an overloaded boat in 2015. Since 2011, more than 5.1 million Syrian refugees, an estimated half of which are children, have fled from civil war in their country.

In recent years Americans have been politically divided over the admission of refugees and asylum seekers as well as the treatment of migrants at the border. Donald Trump was elected president in 2016 in large part by the votes of Americans who want the government to place strict limits on all immigration and reduce the number of refugees and asylum seekers admitted to the country. Others, who believe that the prosperity of the United States should be used to help people from other countries, favor a more welcoming immigration policy, particularly for victims of human rights abuses. The debate over refugees and asylum seekers has been going on for more than seventy years. To understand today's refugee crisis, it is useful to understand how an earlier crisis resulted in the creation of the current system for helping refugees and asylum seekers.

Chapter One

Protecting the Victims of Conflict

Under international law, governments today are responsible for protecting the human rights of their citizens. When a country's government is unable—or unwilling—to do so, citizens may be forced to leave their homes, their families, and their communities to find asylum in another country. Because refugees and asylum seekers are not protected by their own governments, the international community has established ways to help these desperate people by providing shelter, food and clean water, medical care, and opportunities for education and work.

This was not always the case, however. The current system of protections for refugees and asylum seekers was created to resolve a refugee crisis that occurred during World War II. As German armies conquered most of Europe, the Nazi government forced millions of people to work as slave laborers and mandated the mass deportation of, among others, Jews, Poles, and Serbs from many countries. When the European conflict finally ended in 1945 with the defeat of the Nazis, more than 11 million Europeans had been displaced from their homes.

Unwelcoming Attitudes Toward Refugees

Throughout history there have been numerous times when large numbers of people have been forced to flee from war or persecution. But before the 1940s refugees were not entitled to any special protections or consideration. Instead, they were treated like other immigrants. In the United States, for example, more than 20 million immigrants arrived from 1880 to 1920. Unlike previous waves of immigrants, most of whom had come from Great Britain, Ireland, and Germany, most of this new wave were from southern, eastern, and central Europe. About 10 percent of these immigrants were Jewish refugees from eastern Europe, who were fleeing from government-sponsored massacres (known as *pogroms*) in the Russian Empire, which ruled eastern Europe.

The surge in immigration concerned some Americans, who feared that the newcomers would change or harm their society. In 1891 the first federal agency was created to screen immigrants and determine who would be permitted to settle in the country. The Ellis Island Immigration Station was opened the next year in New York Harbor, and immigration officials were stationed at all other US ports of entry. Although millions of immigrants continued to pour into the United States, federal officials began to turn away those who were sick or were considered criminals or potential troublemakers.

World War I and its aftermath led to additional immigration restrictions, as Americans grew concerned that a new wave of refugees would arrive seeking shelter from the conflict in Europe. Legislation passed in 1917 made it harder for immigrants from Europe to gain entry and blocked immigration from most Asian countries altogether. The 1921 Emergency Quota Act established an annual limit of 357,803 immigrants and created a system of national origin quotas that capped the number of immigrants who could be admitted each year from each country. This system was overhauled in 1924 and again in 1929. The changes reduced the total number of annual immigrants to 164,667 and reset the national quotas to favor immigrants from Great Britain.

The year 1929 also marked the start of the Great Depression, a period of economic stagnation that would last through the 1930s. The Depression contributed to anti-immigrant feelings, as

German refugees carrying their belongings wait in line at a train station in 1945. During World War II, more than 11 million Europeans were displaced from their homes.

Americans feared that newcomers would take hard-to-find jobs and resources. The number of immigrants admitted to the United States dropped sharply. From 1925 to 1929, a total of 761,822 immigrants were admitted to the United States—an average of over 152,000 a year. From 1930 to 1934, the total number of immigrants admitted to the United States was 229,301—an average of less than 46,000 a year.

No Place for Refugees

At the same time that the United States and other countries were tightening their immigration laws, political changes in Germany were creating the conditions for a major refugee crisis. Once Adolf Hitler and the Nazi Party gained power in 1933, they began persecuting Jews and other groups. Tragically, those who wished to escape the Nazis often found nowhere to go.

American opinion polls showed that most people did not welcome refugees from Europe. In July 1938 a survey in *Fortune* magazine asked, "What is your attitude toward allowing German, Austrian, and other political refugees to come to the US?" Fewer than 5 percent of respondents favored admitting these refugees, while over 67 percent responded, "With conditions as they are we should try to keep them out."[4]

The United States was not the only country to refuse admission to refugees from Nazi persecution. During the mid- to late 1930s, Great Britain turned away more than five hundred thousand refugees, most of whom were Jewish. France passed laws in 1935 that prohibited Jews from immigrating. Canada, which like the United States was historically considered a safe haven for people fleeing persecution, admitted only five thousand European Jews from 1933 to 1945. "No matter the alarming rhetoric of Hitler's fascist state—and the growing acts of violence against Jews and others—popular sentiment in Western Europe and the United States was largely indifferent to the plight of German Jews,"[5] notes Ishaan Tharoor in the *Washington Post*.

Changing Attitudes

Even before World War II ended, the Allied powers—particularly the United States, Great Britain, France, and the Soviet Union—recognized the need to help refugees. In November 1943, as the Allies were beginning to liberate parts of Europe from Nazi rule, the United States and more than forty other Allied countries established an international organization called the Relief and

> "No matter the alarming rhetoric of Hitler's fascist state—and the growing acts of violence against Jews and others—popular sentiment in Western Europe and the United States was largely indifferent to the plight of German Jews."[5]
>
> —Ishaan Tharoor, journalist

Rehabilitation Administration. Its purpose was to help refugees seeking asylum in Allied territories. The administration provided food, clothing, shelter, and other basic necessities to the victims of war. By the end of the conflict, millions of refugees were living in nearly eight hundred Relief and Rehabilitation Administration camps throughout Europe.

In October 1945 fifty-one countries that had fought together against the Axis powers (Nazi Germany, Italy, and Japan) agreed to form a new organization called the United Nations (UN). The UN's goals were to avoid future wars and to promote peace and justice through international cooperation. The UN soon took over responsibility for helping victims of the world war.

The Tragedy of the *St. Louis*

An example of the challenges faced by Jewish refugees occurred in May 1939 when the German passenger ship *St. Louis* arrived in Cuba. On board were 937 Jewish refugees who had been issued visas to enter Cuba, where they hoped to stay until they were approved to enter the United States. However, after the ship sailed, the Cuban government revoked the visas, fearful that admitting them would encourage additional Jews to come to the island from Europe. When the *St. Louis* arrived in Havana, authorities would not allow the refugees to disembark.

After a week the *St. Louis* sailed for Florida. However, American authorities also refused to allow the ship to land because the refugees had not received US immigration visas. Although the ship passed close enough to the Florida coast that the passengers could see the lights of Miami and Fort Lauderdale, the *St. Louis* was ultimately forced to return to Europe.

The refugees on board were not returned to Germany. Instead, 288 went to Great Britain. Most of the others were admitted to France, Belgium, and the Netherlands. However, in 1940 these three countries were conquered by German armies, leaving most of the *St. Louis* refugees once again subject to Nazi persecution. Nearly all of them ended up in Nazi concentration camps, where more than half of the *St. Louis* refugees died before the war ended.

From the beginning, the United States played a critical role in the UN's activities. In 1946 the United States spearheaded the creation of the UN's International Refugee Organization (IRO), which would replace the wartime Relief and Rehabilitation Administration. The IRO's constitution guaranteed assistance to victims of the Nazi regime and orphans under age sixteen. Over the next five years, the organization helped approximately 8 million European refugees return to their homes. However, millions of refugees still had to resettle in other countries.

The United States did its part in this regard as well. On December 22, 1945, President Harry S. Truman signed an executive order that allowed more than forty thousand European refugees to receive expedited admission into the United States under the existing immigration laws. In 1948 Congress passed a new law, the Displaced Persons Act, which permitted two hundred thousand refugees from Europe to settle permanently in the United States. This legislation was amended in 1950 and 1951 to increase the number of European refugees eligible for resettlement. By 1952 the United States had accepted nearly four hundred thousand refugees—more than 30 percent of the total number resettled by the IRO.

The United Nations High Commissioner for Refugees Is Established

The IRO was intended as a temporary response to the postwar refugee crisis in Europe, but decolonization in Asia and Africa would lead to new waves of refugees not covered under the agency's mandate. The creation of India and Pakistan in 1947 resulted in bitter fighting and 14 million refugees, while the establishment of the Jewish state of Israel in 1948–1949 caused more than 700,000 Palestinians to flee to neighboring Arab lands. These clashes led the UN to recognize the need for a permanent refugee agency. In 1950 the United Nations High Commissioner for Refugees (UNHCR) was established. In July 1951 at a conference in Geneva, Switzerland, twenty-six nations adopted the

Convention Relating to the Status of Refugees, a treaty that provided the legal framework for the UNHCR.

The convention was the first international agreement to formally define what a refugee is. Article I of the 1951 convention defined a refugee as any person who,

> as a result of events occurring before 1 January 1951 and owing to well-founded fear of being persecuted for reasons of race, religion, nationality, membership of a particular social group or political opinion, is outside the country of his nationality and is unable or, owing to such fear, is unwilling to avail himself of the protection of that country; or who, not having a nationality and being outside the country of his former habitual residence . . . is unable or, owing to such fear, is unwilling to return to it.[6]

One of the most important principles introduced in the convention is the principle of non-refoulement. This prevents the governments of countries that host refugees from forcibly returning those who qualify as refugees to their countries of origin.

The 1951 convention did have important limitations, however. For one, its definition only acknowledged those who were refugees prior to 1951. In addition, the signatory nations interpreted the convention to be specifically related to refugees from Europe. This meant that when crises arose in Africa or Asia, the convention's protections did not technically apply. The UNHCR and other UN agencies often provided humanitarian aid in such situations, but over the next two decades it became clear that the problem of refugees would not go away.

US Refugee and Asylum Policy

By the early 1950s the United States and the Soviet Union were engaged in the Cold War, a wide-ranging struggle for influence around the globe. The two superpowers did not fight each other directly but instead sought to enlist other countries as allies

Photographs taken by Nazis show young prisoners in concentration camps. After the war, the United Nations guaranteed assistance to children under the age of sixteen who were orphaned by the Nazi regime.

or, at the very least, to discourage other countries from siding with their adversary. A goal of America's foreign policy was to prevent the spread of communism, so America's refugee policy mainly focused on helping people who were trying to escape from Communist regimes. US leaders believed that this would weaken Communist governments while at the same time helping the victims of communism.

Due to the limitations of the 1951 convention's refugee definition, a new term was used to refer to people fleeing from war or persecution in Communist countries. These people were said to be "seeking asylum." The Refugee Relief Act of 1953 created a new program for those seeking asylum from Communist countries. It allowed for nearly two hundred thousand special immigrant

UN Relief and Works Agency

The region historically known as Palestine is located on the eastern Mediterranean Sea and has been inhabited for millennia by both Arabs and Jews. In May 1948 Jewish settlers in Palestine established the State of Israel, resulting in a war between the Israelis and the Palestinian Arabs, who were supported by neighboring Arab countries. During the two-year conflict, approximately 750,000 Palestinian Arab civilians fled or were forced to leave their homes.

In December 1949 the UN created the UN Relief and Works Agency for Palestine Refugees in the Near East (UNRWA) to help these refugees. Today the agency maintains fifty-eight refugee camps, providing food and basic services to approximately 5.1 million registered Palestinian refugees, as well as operating schools and health clinics. Many of the registered Palestinian refugees are children or grandchildren of the original 1948–1949 refugees. Others are Palestinians who fled from a subsequent June 1967 conflict in which Israel gained control over the largely Palestinian territories known as the West Bank, Gaza Strip, Golan Heights, and East Jerusalem.

The UNRWA's goal is to help the Palestinian refugees until a fair and permanent solution can be found. There has been little progress toward the establishment of an independent Palestinian state, so the UNRWA refugee population continues to grow. Because of this, in August 2018 the administration of President Donald Trump informed the UN that it would no longer provide funding for the UNRWA, arguing that the organization was perpetuating, not helping, the Palestinian refugee crisis.

visas to be issued for refugees; these visas were not subject to the quotas mandated by immigration laws. For example, the United States permitted 2,000 Chinese refugees to immigrate under this program from 1953 to 1956, a time when immigration quotas allowed just 105 Chinese immigrants into the United States annually.

After a failed 1956 uprising in Hungary against its Soviet-backed Communist government, the United States admitted more than thirty-six thousand Hungarian refugees. In 1958 Congress passed a law allowing these Hungarians to become permanent residents of the United States. Over the next two decades, this process would be repeated several times as the United States accepted refugees from other Communist countries, such as Cuba, Vietnam, Cambodia, and Laos.

In 1967 the UN General Assembly amended the convention with a new treaty, the Protocol Relating to the Status of Refugees. The protocol expanded the scope of the 1951 convention by removing the time and geographical limits from the international definition of a refugee. The United States and 145 other countries signed the protocol, which remains in force today.

After accepting more than three hundred thousand refugees fleeing from Communist oppression in Vietnam, Cambo-

Vietnamese refugees are rescued by the US Navy in 1979. After accepting more than three hundred thousand people fleeing from Communist oppression in the late 1970s, the United States finally established a uniform refugee admissions policy.

dia, and Laos during the late 1970s, Congress finally passed legislation to establish a uniform American policy toward refugee admissions. The Refugee Act of 1980 formally incorporated the 1967 protocol definition of a refugee into US law and raised the cap on refugee admissions from 17,400 to 50,000 a year. It also established a new government agency, the Office of Refugee Resettlement, to oversee refugee admissions into the United States. The Refugee Act gives the president the authority to set the annual number of refugee admissions, as well as the power to decide the countries or regions from which refugees will be admitted.

"We cannot avert our eyes or turn our backs. To slam the door in the face of these families would betray our deepest values."[7]

—President Barack Obama

In 1990, processing of asylum claims was separated from other immigration matters after new regulations were added to the Refugee Act. The Immigration and Naturalization Service established an Asylum Corps of specially trained officers who would exclusively work on asylum cases. Today, processing of asylum cases is done by the Asylum Division of the US Citizenship and Immigration Services, which replaced the Immigration and Naturalization Service in 2002.

A Worsening Crisis

As the worldwide refugee and migration crisis has grown worse during the 2010s, world leaders have attempted to find solutions. In September 2016 US president Barack Obama hosted the leaders of more than one hundred countries at a summit in New York City. The event was held concurrently with a UN General Assembly discussion on new ways to help refugees and migrants. "This crisis is a test of our common humanity—whether we give in to suspicion and fear and build walls, or whether we see ourselves in another," Obama said.

> We cannot avert our eyes or turn our backs. To slam the door in the face of these families would betray our deepest values. It would deny our own heritage as nations, including the United States of America, that have been built by immigrants and refugees. And it would be to ignore a teaching at the heart of so many faiths that we do unto others as we would have them do unto us; that we welcome the stranger in our midst. And just as failure to act in the past—for example, by turning away Jews fleeing Nazi Germany—is a stain on our collective conscience, I believe history will judge us harshly if we do not rise to this moment.[7]

Chapter Two

The Dangerous Life of a Refugee

For residents of Homs, a major industrial center of about eight hundred thousand located in western Syria, simply leaving the house became a dangerous ordeal during the spring of 2011. In March and April angry Syrians in Homs and other cities had begun protesting the harsh rule of Bashar al-Assad, demanding that the Syrian dictator relinquish power. The Syrian protests were part of a larger wave of popular uprisings, known as the Arab Spring, that had resulted in the end of long-standing dictatorships in nearby Tunisia, Egypt, and Libya. But unlike the leaders of those countries, Assad refused to step down. Instead, he instructed government forces to fire on demonstrators, killing hundreds of civilians in Homs and elsewhere. Armed Syrians began to fight back against the Assad regime. Soon other groups, including Islamist extremists, had joined the fight to overthrow Assad, and a full-fledged civil war was under way.

The Assad regime cracked down on suspected rebels with increasing brutality. In November 2011 Syrian soldiers rounded up the workers at a sugar factory in Homs, accusing them of supporting the insurgency. Although the soldiers had no proof that the men were rebel sympathizers, they executed them anyway, throwing their bodies into the rubble-strewn street as a warning to those who would challenge the Assad government's authority.

The next day Gasem al-Hamad and his pregnant wife, Wajed, left Homs with their three children. Gasem's brother had been one of the men executed at the sugar factory. A few weeks earlier another one of Gasem's brothers had been killed by a bomb that government forces dropped on his neighborhood in Homs. Wajed's brother had also been killed in the conflict. Gasem and Wajed moved their family to Palmyra, a city in Syria that is about three hours away, where they could live with relatives.

People who leave their homes to escape violence but who remain within the borders of their county are known as internally displaced persons (IDPs). Like Gasem and Wajed, millions of other Syrians were internally displaced as a result of the civil war. However, staying within the country is not necessarily safe. Under international law, the Syrian government was still responsible for helping IDPs, rather than international organizations like the UNHCR.

For Gasem and Wajed, there was little chance that they would ever return to their old home. After they arrived in Palmyra, friends from Homs sent photos showing that their house had been destroyed by a bomb. As the fighting in Syria continued, Gasem and Wajed decided they were not safe in Palmyra either. After a few months they decided to flee Syria altogether.

Reaching a Safe Country

The journey to a safe country can be long and dangerous due to natural hazards or bad weather, food or water shortages, and challenging terrain. Sometimes, refugees must travel on foot or in makeshift boats and find shelter along their route. Refugees often have to deal with human hazards as well, such as accidentally straying into areas where military forces are active, or being attacked and robbed by predatory thugs. There is also an ever-present danger of being caught by authorities, who may imprison or execute them.

Refugees often cross borders illegally. Under normal circumstances, a person who wants to travel to another country must have a passport and usually a visa granting them permission to enter. However, it is nearly impossible for refugees fleeing combat zones to obtain visas, mostly because when conflicts begin, most foreign embassies withdraw their staffs, who are responsible for processing such documents.

In Syria, legal international travel was not an option for Gasem and Wajed. Instead, they paid most of their remaining money to smugglers, who promised to help them avoid government checkpoints and cross the Syrian border into Jordan. Gasem and Wajed made it across the border and in April 2012 arrived at the Jordanian city of Al Mafraq, where they could stay with relatives.

Angry Syrians began protesting the harsh rule of Syria's dictator Bashar al-Assad in 2011. The Syrian protests were part of a larger wave of uprisings known as the Arab Spring.

Soon after arriving, Gasem and Wajed visited a UN office in Jordan's capital, Amman, where they formally registered as refugees. UN officials held an in-depth interview with the couple then conducted background checks to confirm that they were eligible for asylum. Once Gasem and Wajed showed that their plight was legitimate, the family would be allowed to stay in Jordan and receive help.

Registration of refugees helps the UNHCR as well as the host country's officials and nongovernmental organizations plan appropriately to care for the refugees. This enables them to determine the appropriate amounts of shelter, food, water, health and sanitation facilities, and financial aid that will be needed. Registration also helps weed out people who are trying to defraud the system or are involved in human trafficking. Refugees benefit as well. Once refugees are registered, some host countries will issue them identity documents, which show that they are legally allowed to be in the country. In some cases these documents give refugees greater freedom of movement within the host country or permit them to find work, open a bank account, or rent a home.

Life in a Refugee Camp

After being processed, refugees are settled in new homes within the host country. Often, camps are created to accommodate large numbers of refugees. Many of these camps are located on the outskirts of urban areas. The government of the country that is hosting the refugees sets up the camps, but they are usually managed by the UNHCR, with aid from international organizations such as the Red Cross, Oxfam, and the United Nations Children's Fund.

Although 85 percent of refugee camps are located in developed nations, some camps are located in less developed countries that can barely feed, clothe, and shelter their own people, much less support a large population of refugees. This is the case in Cameroon (which hosts refugees from the Central African Republic), Uganda (home to refugees from South Sudan), and Chad (home to refugees from the Darfur region of Sudan.) Additionally, because the camps are often located near the border of the country where conflict has produced refugees, the camps are vulnerable to attack. In May 2016, for example, Syrian combatants bombed the al-Kamouna refugee camp near the Turkey-Syria border, killing at least thirty people. (Both government and rebel forces claimed the other side had carried out the attack.)

Life in a refugee camp can be disorienting and traumatic as refugees try to adjust to a new way of life. UNHCR workers often set up schools and other social activities to help children adjust. However, despite the best efforts of aid workers, conditions in refugee camps tend to be appalling. Many refugees are sick or hurt when they arrive. The camps have limited medical facilities, and poor sanitation is common, so the risk of disease and infection is high. Living conditions are squalid and overcrowded and provide little privacy for families, many of whom fear for the safety of their children and women. "I started to cry to myself about the situation after the first three days," commented one Syrian refugee living in the Zaatari camp in Jordan. "How could things come to this?"[8]

Living Outside a Refugee Camp

As a result of the poor conditions in refugee camps, many refugees look to leave the camps as soon as they can. In 2019 the UN estimated that over 70 percent of the global refugee population lived in apartment-type private housing with their families. Most of these refugees are in urban areas of developing countries like Jordan or Turkey.

Living outside a camp places a significant economic burden on refugees. In the camp, they receive food, water, shelter, and medical care funded by the UNHCR. When refugees are granted permission to live outside the camp, they remain eligible for certain benefits, including food

"I started to cry to myself about the situation after the first three days. How could things come to this?"[8]

—A Syrian refugee in the Zaatari camp in Jordan

Internally Displaced Persons

Not all people forced to leave their homes are able or willing to leave their countries. Instead, some people resettle temporarily in safer areas within their country. Such people are known as internally displaced persons, or IDPs. In 2019 the UNHCR estimated that more than 41 million people were internally displaced due to armed conflicts, human rights violations, or natural disasters such as floods or typhoons.

Remaining within their home country may sound more appealing than becoming a refugee. However, there are important differences between IDPs and refugees. Once refugees have crossed their country's border, they are entitled to certain protections under international law and can receive help from the UNHCR, the Red Cross, and other aid agencies. On the other hand, IDPs remain under the jurisdiction of their country's government, which limits the amount of assistance that international organizations can provide. IDPs depend on their government to protect them from violence—even though, in some cases, that government is causing the violence that forced them to leave their homes in the first place. "The overwhelming majority of internally displaced persons are women and children," notes the Office of the United Nations High Commissioner for Human Rights. "More often than refugees, the internally displaced tend to remain close to or become trapped in zones of conflict, caught in the cross-fire and at risk of being used as pawns, targets or human shields by the belligerents."

Office of the United Nations High Commissioner for Human Rights, "Questions and Answers About IDPs." www.ohchr.org.

rations and modest stipends for housing and travel. However, due to limited budgets and rising demand, this assistance is usually not enough to fully cover the expenses of a family living outside the camp, so once they go out on their own, refugees must find a way to earn money for rent and food. Although living outside of UNHCR camps can be a challenge, some refugee families are so discouraged by conditions in the camp that they simply leave without permission. They try to blend in to the society of the host country and forgo additional support from the UNHCR or other organizations.

Finding affordable housing is a major challenge. Syrian refugees Gasem and Wajed did not have to stay in the Zaatari refugee camp in Jordan because they could live with relatives in the nearby city of Al Mafraq. The experience of another Syrian, Abdel Salam, is more typical. After escaping from Syria into neighboring Lebanon in 2017, Abdel and his family registered as refugees and settled in Tripoli, a city of about three hundred thousand people. They found a small, unheated apartment for $156 a month. However, like many refugees, Abdel struggled to find work. As an unskilled laborer, he could only earn about $175 a month, which had to cover food for the family, fuel, and medical care in addition to the monthly rent. Assistance from the UNHCR helped cover Abdel's living expenses.

Children play in a Syrian refugee camp in Turkey in 2015. Living conditions at refugee camps in underdeveloped countries are often squalid, overcrowded, and do not provide enough food for people.

Often, host countries do not grant refugees in urban areas permission to work, because the authorities do not want them to settle permanently in the country. Jordanian and Lebanese authorities have taken identity documents away from Syrian refugees to prevent them from getting legitimate jobs. To support their families, refugees like Gasem and Abdel must often work for businesses willing to pay them secretly because they do not have the proper work papers. Such jobs generally involve hard or dangerous labor, low wages, and few benefits. There is also the threat that refugees caught working illegally can be forced to give up their private apartments and return to the camp.

Even doctors, lawyers, and other white-collar professionals usually find themselves unable to work in their previous fields when they become refugees. "In Syria, I was an engineer . . . working for a Japanese company," recounted a refugee named Najib.

> International companies in Turkey told me that I have to be a Turkish citizen to give me work. Despite this, I worked for one year at night for a small Turkish company, working from 7 PM TO 5 AM. . . . My boss didn't want to help me get a work permit, because the boss would have to pay for the permit and insurance. . . . Instead they gave me work at night and a low salary. I was paid 2,200 Lira ($733) and Turkish people doing the same job earned 8,000 Lira ($2,667).[9]

Najib ended up working in a restaurant, rather than trying to find another engineering job.

Resettlement

Refugee camps are supposed to provide a temporary safety net, but most of the conflicts that produce refugees cannot be quickly or easily resolved. Repatriation, or returning to one's home country once the threat has ended, might take years—or never even be possible. As of 2019 the average length of stay in a refugee camp was more than twelve years. Such long stays in refugee camps are good for no one. Elizabeth Cullen Dunn writes in the *Boston Review*:

> When people stay for so long, the bareness of camps, their lack of services, and their segregation from the surrounding society become chronic problems. Camps keep refugees alive, but they prevent them from living. Most camps lack schools, places of worship, and shops. Even when donors such as the United Nations or the Turkish government create camps with more permanent infrastructure, most lack the amenities a town of equivalent size would [offer].[10]

Options for addressing the slow pace of repatriation are limited. One option is allowing refugees to live permanently in the country that has provided safe haven. However, many of these countries worry about sudden dramatic increases in their population and therefore object to this idea. Another option is the relocation of refugees to a third country.

When the UNHCR identifies refugees whose specific needs cannot be met in their country of asylum, it has the option to refer their cases for permanent resettlement in another country. A refugee accepted for resettlement is granted permanent resident status in a new country, including the eventual opportunity to become a citizen of that country. In 2018 twenty-seven countries around the world accepted 55,680 refugees for resettlement, including the United States (17,100), Canada (7,700), the United Kingdom (5,700),

"When people stay for so long, the bareness of camps, their lack of services, and their segregation from the surrounding society become chronic problems. Camps keep refugees alive, but they prevent them from living."[10]

—Elizabeth Cullen Dunn, journalist

A Syrian mother prepares a meal for her young son at a refugee camp. As of 2019 the average length of stay in a refugee camp was more than twelve years.

France (5,100), and Sweden (4,900). "Though not an option for the vast majority of refugees," notes William Swing, director general of the International Organization for Migration, "resettlement gives real hope and a chance to begin life anew to many who would otherwise have neither home nor country to call their own."[11]

The process of resettlement in the United States is more stringent than that of most other countries. Refugees undergo health checks, repeated biometric verification of their identity via fingerprints and photographs, several layers of biographical and background screening, and multiple in-person interviews with immigration and law enforcement officials. The entire process usually takes eighteen to twenty-four months and occurs in the country where the refugee has received asylum.

One Family's Experience

When they sought refugee status in the United States, Gasem and Wajed al-Hamad recounted numerous meetings and interviews, some of which lasted longer than ten hours. "They want to know

UNHCR Goodwill Ambassadors

Since the early 1950s the UN has asked prominent celebrities to serve as goodwill ambassadors who are charged with drawing public attention to important issues. UNHCR goodwill ambassadors come from many countries. In 2019 they included Alek Wek, a former Sudanese refugee turned supermodel; British writer Neil Gaiman; Uruguayan actor Osvaldo Laport; Chinese activist Yao Chen; and Spanish television star Jesús Vázquez.

Among the best-known UN advocates for refugees and asylum seekers is actress Angelina Jolie. Appointed a goodwill ambassador in 2001, Jolie has visited UNHCR facilities in more than fifty countries, investigating living conditions for refugees. She has also spent over $5 million of her own money to help fund schools for refugees in Kenya, Afghanistan, and other locations. In 2005 Jolie started the National Center for Refugee and Immigrant Children, which provides free legal aid to young asylum seekers. Due to the wide-ranging scope of her efforts, in 2011 the UNHCR designated Jolie as its first special envoy. In this position, Jolie represents the UNHCR in international discussions on refugee matters.

In a UNHCR speech on World Refugee Day in 2009, Jolie commented:

> As an American I know the strength that diversity has given my country—a country built by what now some would dismiss as asylum seekers or economic migrants—and I believe we must persuade the world that refugees must not be simply viewed as a burden. They are the survivors. And they can bring those qualities to the service of their communities and the countries that shelter them.

Quoted in Andrew Purvis, "World Refugee Day: Angelina Jolie Calls for Greater Understanding of the Plight of Refugees," United Nations High Commissioner for Refugees, June 18, 2009. www.unhcr.org.

everything about your life, your family. Everything," recalled Gasem. "Do you have tattoos, wounds on your body?" were some questions he recalled. Others included, "When did your dad die? And your mom? Were you in the army? When did you serve? Where?"[12]

Finally, in December 2014 the family received permission to resettle in the United States. Their case was turned over to the

International Rescue Committee, one of nine nongovernmental organizations that work with the UNHCR to manage resettlement within the United States. The International Rescue Committee arranged for Gasem and Wajed to receive US Permanent Residence Cards, often called "green cards," which show that they are allowed to live and work in the United States. The organization also made travel arrangements to bring the family to America and identified a community where they could be permanently settled within the country.

On February 9, 2015, the family arrived in Turlock, California, a city of seventy-two thousand located about 100 miles (161 km) southeast of San Francisco. Gasem soon found a job at a slaughterhouse, doing the same sort of work that he had done in Syria. He and Wajed found a place to worship at a local mosque, and their children have adapted and done well in the local schools. In 2019 they celebrated the birth of their fifth child, and Gasem received a promotion that enabled the family to move out of their small apartment into a larger house. In 2020, having lived legally in the United States for five years, they can apply for US citizenship.

Gasem and Wajed are among approximately thirty-five thousand Syrian refugees who have found a safe home in the United States since the civil war began in their country. However, there remain nearly 26 million refugees who have not yet been able to permanently resettle in another country. And changing immigration policies in the United States over the past few years may take away the chance for those refugees ever to come to America.

Chapter Three

Resettling Refugees in the United States

The United States has long been a haven for refugees from all over the world. Over the past forty years, about 3 million refugees have resettled in the United States under a program created by the Refugee Act of 1980. This represents more than 70 percent of the total number of resettled refugees worldwide in that period. The United States accepts more refugees per year than any other country, and until recently, the United States resettled more refugees per year than the rest of the world's countries combined.

But since the inauguration of Donald Trump as president in January 2017, there has been a sharp reduction in the number of refugees admitted to the United States, as well as major changes in the ways that people who seek asylum are treated by federal authorities. This dramatic shift in US policy has affected the families of Gasem al-Hamad and other Syrian refugees who have already resettled in the United States. Gasem's older brother and nephew followed his lead by escaping from Syria into Jordan, and in 2016 US authorities approved both for resettlement in the United States. The nephew arrived in the United States in December 2016; he lived with Gasem's family in California for a few months, then found his own apartment. But during Trump's first week in office, the president issued a travel ban that prevented people from Syria and other Muslim countries from entering the United States. By the time the ban was lifted, the Trump administration had imposed tighter restrictions on the admission of refugees from Muslim countries like Syria, as well as on all asylum seekers. This shift in US policy has left Gasem's brother stuck in Jordan despite his resettlement authorization.

Presidential Control over Refugee Admissions

The Refugee Act of 1980, which established the current US system overseeing refugee admissions, gives the president authority to determine how many refugees will be admitted to the country each year. Historically, the refugee limit has fluctuated depending on events around the world. In 1980–1981 more than two hundred thousand refugees were admitted each year; many were Cubans who came during a mass emigration from Cuba known as the Mariel boatlift. Refugee admissions dropped over the next few years but rose again to exceed one hundred thousand a year from 1989 to 1995 in response to a new refugee crisis in Europe. This crisis was triggered by the fall of the Berlin Wall, the collapse of the Soviet Union, and the breakup of Yugoslavia, which resulted in conflicts throughout the Balkan Peninsula.

As president from 2001 to 2009, George W. Bush established the limit on refugees at 70,000 a year; in the last year of his term, Bush raised the limit to 80,000. Throughout the Bush years, however, the United States never accepted the full number of refugees allowed, in part due to security concerns after the al Qaeda terrorist attacks on September 11, 2001. From 2002 to 2008 about 312,000 refugees were resettled in the United States, an average of about 44,500 per year.

When Barack Obama was elected president, the refugee cap remained at 80,000. However, the United States accepted more refugees per year during the Obama years. Refugee admissions jumped from 60,191 in 2008 (Bush's final year in office) to 74,654 and 73,311 in 2009 and 2010 (Obama's first two years in office).

For 2013 Obama lowered the refugee limit to 70,000, where it would stay for the next three years. However, as the number of refugees grew worldwide due to ongoing conflicts in Syria, Iraq,

In 2015, this young Syrian boy's body was found washed ashore in Turkey after the small refugee boat his family was on sank. The shocking image drew widespread attention and horror to the growing refugee crisis.

Afghanistan, and Africa, the Obama administration accepted the full quota of 70,000 refugees each year.

Global Crisis Leads to Increased Resettlement

The year 2015 marked the point when the refugee problem became a full-blown international crisis. That year, nearly 1 million refugees and migrants tried to reach Europe, prompting heated political debates in many countries. Most of the refugees and migrants were trying to reach the Schengen Area, a group of countries within the European Union that have eliminated their border controls. Germany, Hungary, Sweden, and Austria were among the most popular destinations in the area for refugees.

In hopes of reaching these countries, refugees took to the seas and then planned to travel overland. One of the main routes involved African refugees crossing the Mediterranean Sea from Libya to Italy or from Morocco to Spain or Malta. Another major route was taken by Syrian refugees who left Turkey and tried to reach Greece in small boats. Thousands of refugees died on these journeys, including three-year-old Aylan Kurdi. In September 2015 a shocking photo of Alyan's lifeless body on a beach in Turkey, where it had washed ashore after the small boat his family was traveling in sank, appeared in newspapers and other media around the world. It drew widespread attention to the refugee crisis. Public opinion in favor of humanitarian intervention compelled European governments to accept more refugees and ensure their safety.

Horrified Americans, as well as overwhelmed European governments, asked the United States to take more refugees from Syria. They noted that while the United States had resettled more than 250,000 refugees from 2011 to 2015, only about 2,000 were Syrians. Obama responded by raising the refugee cap for 2016 to 85,000 and publicly setting a goal of resettling at least 10,000 Syrians during that year.

Growing Concerns

While some human rights advocates complained that the ten thousand figure was too low, many other Americans were uneasy about the proposal due to growing fears about terrorism. During 2015 terrorists affiliated with the Syrian group Islamic State of Iraq and the Levant (ISIL) had carried out attacks in cities throughout Europe. On November 13, 2015, two months after Obama's refugee commitment, ISIL terrorists conducted a series of coordinated bombings and mass shootings that left 130 people dead and more than 365 wounded in Paris.

Four days after the Paris attack, legislation that would require the FBI and the US Department of Homeland Security (DHS) to conduct a more stringent scrutiny of Syrian and Iraqi refugees was introduced in the House of Representatives. The American SAFE Act of 2015 passed in the House but failed in the Senate. However, members of both parties backed a temporary pause in refugee admissions until processes could be reviewed and strengthened to prevent terrorists from entering the country.

State and local officials also voiced concerns about Obama's Syrian resettlement goals. By November 17, 2015, the governors of thirty states had told the White House that they did not want refugees resettled in their states. And a poll by the Gallup organization taken on November 23 found that 60 percent of Americans opposed Obama's proposal to take in ten thousand more Syrian refugees, while just 37 percent supported the plan.

Heightened Controversy

Donald Trump soon jumped into the fray. Trump had made restricting immigration a central element of his campaign. In campaign speeches and interviews, he had played on fears that "outsiders" from Mexico and Central America would come into America and change or destroy the culture. Now Trump targeted Muslim refugees, saying that if elected he would restrict them from entering the United States. In a November 2015 interview with conservative commentator Sean Hannity, Trump referred to Syrian refugees as "the ultimate Trojan horse," suggesting that terrorists were disguising themselves as refugees to get into the United States and wreak havoc. "We should do maybe a safe zone or something over in Syria and get everybody else involved and have a big safe zone," Trump said. "But I tell you, if they come into this country, they're going out. If I win, they're going out. We can't take a chance."[13]

Media outlets and the Obama administration pushed back against Trump's claims. "If a potential terrorist is determined to enter America to do harm, there are easier and faster ways to get there than by going through the complex refugee resettlement process,"[14]

"If a potential terrorist is determined to enter America to do harm, there are easier and faster ways to get there than by going through the complex refugee resettlement process."[14]

—V.V.B., editorial writer for the *Economist*

noted an essay in the *Economist*. And *Washington Post* fact-checker Michelle Ye Hee Lee reported,

> A State Department spokesperson said of the nearly 785,000 refugees admitted through the US Refugee Admissions Program since 9/11, "only about a dozen—a tiny fraction of one percent of admitted refugees—have been arrested or removed from the US due to terrorism concerns that existed prior to their resettlement in the US. None of them were Syrian."[15]

Despite the controversy, the refugee resettlement program was not halted. The American SAFE Act failed to pass in the Senate, but the Obama administration eased some concerns by tightening the screening process for refugee admissions. The initial pace of Syrian resettlement was slow, due to the enhanced screening process, but by the end of 2016, the United States had resettled 12,587 Syrian refugees, among a total of 84,988 refugees from all countries.

Although his term as president was ending, Obama proposed that the limit on refugee admissions should be increased again for 2017, to 110,000. He also declared his support for resettling at least 10,000 more Syrians during that year. However,

Tragic and Iconic Photo

Abdullah and Reyhana Kurdi were among the more than 1 million desperate refugees and migrants who tried to reach Europe during 2015. The Kurdis fled from Syria to Turkey in 2012 when the ruthless Islamic State of Iraq and Syria (ISIS) took control of their village. The Kurdis hoped to eventually resettle with their two children, five-year-old Galip and three-year-old Aylan, in Canada, where some relatives lived. The Turkish government would not let the Kurdis leave, but they could no longer tolerate the poor living conditions and lack of job opportunities in the refugee camp. So they engaged smugglers to get them to Europe.

The smugglers arranged for the family and twelve other migrants to cross the Aegean Sea to Greece in an inflatable rubber raft. The raft, designed to hold eight people, was unsuitable for ocean travel. Soon after setting out, high waves filled the overloaded raft with water and it capsized, plunging the migrants into the sea. "We had no life vests," Abdullah later told Turkish reporters. "People panicked when water filled the boat and it sank. . . . My children slipped from my grasp."

Abdullah was one of four passengers who survived. Some of the drowned passengers washed up on a nearby beach, including Abdullah's son Aylan. A Turkish journalist's photograph of the drowned toddler was broadcast and printed around the world. For many people, the tragic image encapsulated the desperation of refugees, as well as the dangerous choices that families are often forced to make in order to find safety.

Quoted in Laura King and Glen Johnson, "Death of Syrian Toddler Throws Global Spotlight onto Refugee Crisis," *Los Angeles Times*, September 3, 2015. www.latimes.com.

At the end of his term as president, Barack Obama proposed that the limit on refugee admissions should be increased to 110,000. He also declared his support for resettling at least 10,000 more Syrians in 2016.

changing political currents would result in a swift reversal in US refugee policy.

Closing the Door

Just days after being inaugurated as the forty-fifth president of the United States, Trump began acting on his promises to restrict immigration and refugee admissions. On January 27, 2017, he signed Executive Order 13769, which prevented travel to the United States from seven predominantly Muslim countries (Iran, Iraq, Libya, Somalia, Sudan, Syria, and Yemen) and suspended the US refugee admission program for 120 days. The executive order directed government agencies to review the refugee vetting processes of other countries during this period to ensure that they were "adequate to ensure the security and welfare of the

United States Not the First Choice for Syrian Refugees

Both Donald Trump and his predecessor Barack Obama have been criticized at times by the international community for not doing enough to help Syrian refugees. Yet a survey conducted by the Gallup organization in November 2015 found that relatively few Syrians were interested in resettling permanently in the United States. "Although Gallup surveys since 2007 have shown that the United States is the top desired destination for potential migrants worldwide and that Northern America (which includes the United States and Canada) is the most desired region, only 6 percent of potential migrants in Syria desired to migrate to either of these areas," wrote the poll authors.

According to the poll, 46 percent of the respondents said that, if given the opportunity, they would prefer to move permanently to another country. The most popular potential destination was Europe, chosen by 39 percent of respondents. The Middle East and North Africa, where societies are predominantly Muslim, was the preference for 35 percent of those polled. Ten percent wished to resettle in Asia, while just 6 percent chose to resettle in the United States or Canada.

Nader Nekvasil and Mohamed Yours, "Nearly Half of Syrians Would Leave Syria If They Could," Gallup, November 30, 2015. https://news.gallup.com.

United States."[16] The order also specifically blocked Syrian refugees from entering the country and reduced the cap on refugee admissions for 2017 from 110,000 to 50,000.

Trump's executive order—dubbed in news stories as the Muslim travel ban—went into effect the day it was issued, creating chaos and confusion. Hundreds of travelers from the targeted countries were detained at border control checkpoints in airports and other ports of entry. Even some naturalized citizens who had been visiting relatives in one of the blocked countries were not permitted to return to their homes in the United States. Over the next few weeks, up to sixty thousand foreigners had their visas revoked.

The ban was immediately challenged in court. Several states filed lawsuits to block implementation of the order, as did some naturalized US citizens from the affected countries who were prevented by the ban from reentering the United States. In February a federal district court judge ruled in *State of Washington v. Trump* that the government could not implement the order, a decision that was confirmed by the Ninth Circuit Court of Appeals.

Thwarted, Trump revoked the order on March 6, 2017, and replaced it with Executive Order 13780, a similar ban crafted to survive the legal challenges that had sunk the original order. The indefinite ban on Syrian refugees was replaced with a freeze on all refugee admissions for 120 days, so the Trump administration could review admissions policies and procedures. Iraq was dropped from the list of countries whose citizens could not enter the United States, while people from the other six countries were blocked from receiving US visas for 90 days. The order also required all refugees to receive a visa before entering the country and dropped language that many observers felt favored the admission of Christian refugees over Muslims.

Refugee advocates quickly criticized the revised travel ban, arguing that it penalized refugees without improving security. "President Trump still seems to believe you can determine who's a terrorist by knowing which country a man, woman or child is from," said Grace Meng, an immigration researcher with Human Rights Watch. "Putting this executive order into effect will only create a false sense of security that genuine steps are being taken to protect Americans from attack, while undermining the standing of the US as a refuge for those at greatest risk."[17]

Once again, numerous lawsuits were filed challenging the constitutionality of Executive Order 13780. On June 24 the US Supreme Court ruled that parts of the order could go into effect, including the four-month freeze on refugee admissions.

"President Trump still seems to believe you can determine who's a terrorist by knowing which country a man, woman or child is from."[17]

—Grace Meng, immigration researcher with Human Rights Watch

On October 24, as the freeze expired, Trump issued a new executive order restarting the refugee admissions program with new policies, procedures, and security enhancements. Refugees that the US Department of State believes present a security risk to the United States are subject to more stringent review and admitted on a case-by-case basis.

New Policies Take Effect

As a result of the new policies, just 53,716 refugees were admitted to the United States during 2017, less than half of the previous administration's limit. Despite the restrictions, 6,557 of these refugees were from Syria, making them the third-largest group admitted after refugees from the Democratic Republic of the Congo (9,377) and Iraq (6,886). Many of the Syrians and Iraqis were admitted before Trump took office or during the months when courts blocked the implementation of his travel bans.

For 2018 Trump reduced the cap on refugee admissions to 45,000—the lowest level ever under the Refugee Act of 1980. As his new policies continued to take hold, the number of refugee admissions continued to drop. During 2018 only 22,491 refugees were resettled in the United States. The top five countries of origin were the Democratic Republic of the Congo, Myanmar, Ukraine, Bhutan, and Eritrea. Just 62 Syrians and 140 Iraqis were resettled within the United States during 2018. "This administration's decision to halve the number of refugees admitted to America is a double-blow—to victims of war ready to start a new life, and to America's reputation as a beacon of hope in the world," complained David Miliband, a former British foreign secretary who now heads the International Rescue Committee. "When America cuts its numbers, the danger is that it sets the stage for other nations to follow suit, a tragic and contagious example of moral failure."[18]

Despite the complaints, Trump further reduced the refugee admissions limit for 2019, setting a new cap of thirty thousand resettlements. The reduction was justified by US officials, including Secretary of State Mike Pompeo, who contended that the United States could not accept more refugees from abroad while simultaneously dealing with a surge of asylum seekers at its south-western border. "This year's refugee ceiling reflects the substantial increase in the num-ber of individuals seeking asylum in our country, leading to a massive backlog of outstanding asy-lum cases and greater public expense,"[19] explained Pompeo.

In September 2019 the Trump administration an-nounced that it would reduce the cap on refugee resettle-ments to eighteen thousand. This was by far the lowest limit in the history of the program, and marked a 40 percent reduc-tion from the previous year.

"This year's refugee ceiling reflects the substantial increase in the number of individuals seeking asylum in our country, leading to a massive backlog of outstanding asylum cases and greater public expense."[19]

—US secretary of state Mike Pompeo

Chapter Four

A Broken Asylum System

In June 2019 a shocking image appeared in many American newspapers and media outlets. The photo showed the drowned bodies of a young man from El Salvador, Óscar Alberto Martínez Ramírez, and his toddler daughter, Angie Valeria, floating in the shallow water of the Rio Grande, which marks the border between Mexico and Texas. The not-quite-two-year-old girl was still clinging to her father's neck. They had died while trying to cross the river so they could request asylum in the United States.

For many people, this tragic photograph represented the desperation of millions of Central Americans who have fled poverty and violence in their home countries over the past decades. The Martínez family had been waiting in a migrant camp on the Mexican side of the border for their turn to present themselves to US authorities and request asylum. But a new policy known as metering has drastically slowed the rate at which asylum cases are processed at the border, leaving families waiting in Mexico for months. Some migrants give up and return home when their money runs out. Others, like Martínez, try to cross the border illegally, hoping that once inside the United States they will be permitted to stay while their asylum request is processed.

But even if he had survived the crossing, Martínez probably would not have qualified for asylum. Like most migrants, he had traveled north seeking better economic prospects in the

United States. His mother told reporters that he had hoped to live and work in the United States for a few years so that his family could save enough money to return to El Salvador and build a home of their own. Although El Salvador has high levels of gang-related violence and political corruption, US authorities probably would have determined that Martínez was an economic migrant, not a refugee. "Refugees have different legal rights than economic migrants," explains David Miliband, president of the International Rescue Committee. "People fleeing economic collapse, famine or climate change certainly have a claim to international aid and protection, but they are not the same as people for whom religion, ethnicity or political affiliation directly puts their life at risk."[20]

Nonetheless, today there are approximately twenty thousand asylum seekers like Martínez and his family who are living in shabby camps along the US-Mexico border, waiting for their asylum requests to be considered. Millions of others are already living in the United States while waiting for their claims to be processed.

Requesting Asylum

There are significant differences between the refugee resettlement program and the asylum program. Refugees who wish to be resettled in the United States must apply outside the country, where they are thoroughly vetted before being allowed to enter. The asylum process cannot begin until the applicant is physically present in the United States. Another difference is that there is no cap or limit on the number of people who can be granted asylum in the United States in a given year.

Some asylum seekers begin a process called *affirmative asylum* once they enter the United States. It does not matter whether they entered legally on a

"People fleeing economic collapse, famine or climate change certainly have a claim to international aid and protection, but they are not the same as people for whom religion, ethnicity or political affiliation directly puts their life at risk."[20]

—David Miliband, president of the International Rescue Committee

Salvadoran migrant Óscar Alberto Martínez Ramírez and his toddler-age daughter, Angie Valeria, drowned while trying to cross the Rio Grande River into Texas. Ramírez was seeking asylum for his family and had grown frustrated by weeks of waiting.

travel visa or crossed the border illegally. So long as they have been in the country for less than a year, such individuals can present themselves to immigration officials and request asylum. After completing an application, an asylum seeker is fingerprinted and information is taken for a background check.

Next the asylum seeker is interviewed by a US Citizenship and Immigration Services (USCIS) asylum officer. To qualify for asylum, the USCIS states, the person must be able to show the officer that there is a "'significant possibility' . . . that he or she has been persecuted or has a well-founded fear of persecution or harm on account of his or her race, religion, nationality, membership in a particular social group, or political opinion if returned to his or her country."[21] If the asylum officer determines that the person meets the credible fear standard, the migrant is granted asylum and is permitted to remain in the country legally. The United States typically grants asylum to about twenty thousand to twenty-five thousand people annually.

Like other refugees, those granted asylum receive government documents that allow them to work and apply for a driver's license. A year after being granted asylum, a person can seek to change his or her immigration status and become a permanent resident. This entitles an asylee to additional benefits, such as accruing time toward the five years required to be

Asylum Seekers and Legal Representation

The likelihood that a migrant will obtain asylum is much higher if he or she can afford a lawyer to help with the case. In 2017, 90 percent of asylum applicants who did not have a lawyer were denied asylum, while almost half of those who had legal representation succeeded in receiving asylum. But unlike criminal cases, in which defendants are entitled to legal counsel even if they cannot afford it, the US government does not provide legal assistance to asylum seekers.

For most migrants, navigating the system is challenging. Those who do not read English can easily be confused by the forms they are required to fill out and submit. Some migrants have been scheduled for deportation simply because they did not understand when paperwork had to be filed or when hearings were scheduled. The USCIS provides a website for those who have Internet access; however, it includes relatively few resources to help migrants who do not understand the system.

"For many people in immigration proceedings, a deportation order is a death sentence. Worse still, our immigration system is a labyrinth that is difficult for even seasoned attorneys to navigate," says Madhuri Grewal, an immigration policy attorney with the American Civil Liberties Union. The organization has long pushed for legal representation for people faced with deportation. At the very least, the organization contends, this assures a fair hearing.

Quoted in Congressman Anthony Brown, "ACLU Endorses Rep. Brown's Equal Justice for Immigrants Act," July 22, 2019. https://anthonybrown.house.gov.

eligible for US citizenship. There is a waiting list, however, since only ten thousand asylees are granted permanent resident status each year.

If an asylum officer determines that a person does not meet the credible fear criterion, the asylum request is denied and the migrant's immigration status is checked. If the person entered the country legally, he or she can remain until his or her visa expires. If the person came illegally or has already overstayed his or her visa, the case is referred to the US Immigration and Customs Enforcement or the US Customs and Border Protection (CBP) for deportation from the country.

People who are scheduled to be deported because their affirmative asylum request was denied or migrants who were caught trying to enter the United States illegally can use the *defensive asylum* process to remain in the country. This gives the person an opportunity to present his or her case before an immigration judge. Unlike the affirmative asylum interview, the hearing is adversarial, so a USCIS attorney represents the government and attacks the asylee's case through cross-examination. The asylee must prove that he or she meets the credible fear standard to qualify for asylum under US law. When both sides have been heard, the immigration judge will either order the USCIS to grant asylum or order the individual to be removed from the United States. Deportation is usually not immediate, and migrants can remain in the United States while appealing the judge's decision.

Severe Backlog

Only about 20 percent of asylees are ultimately granted permission to stay in the United States. This is because it is hard to meet the standard to receive asylum. There might be little doubt that an applicant has fled from a terrible situation. The person may truly expect to be harmed or even killed in his or her country. But unless the threat of violence is motivated by the person's membership in one of the protected classes of refugees, that person has no legal right to protection in the United States.

What Should the Top Priorities Be for Dealing with Asylum Seekers?

When asked about the situation at the US-Mexico border, a majority of Americans say the top priorities should be adding more judges to handle asylum cases and providing safe, sanitary conditions for asylum seekers. The next highest priority, according to the poll, is reducing the number of people seeking asylum in the United States. These are among the findings of a Pew Research Center poll conducted between July 22 and August 4, 2019.

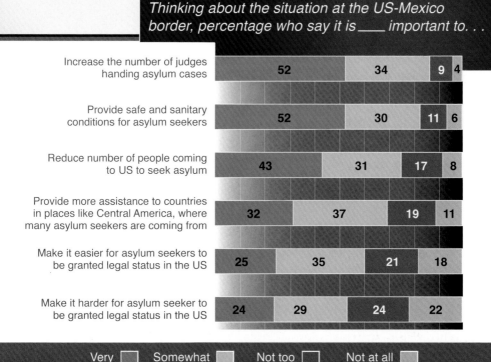

Thinking about the situation at the US-Mexico border, percentage who say it is ____ important to. . .

	Very	Somewhat	Not too	Not at all
Increase the number of judges handing asylum cases	52	34	9	4
Provide safe and sanitary conditions for asylum seekers	52	30	11	6
Reduce number of people coming to US to seek asylum	43	31	17	8
Provide more assistance to countries in places like Central America, where many asylum seekers are coming from	32	37	19	11
Make it easier for asylum seekers to be granted legal status in the US	25	35	21	18
Make it harder for asylum seeker to be granted legal status in the US	24	29	24	22

Very ▢ Somewhat ▢ Not too ▢ Not at all ▢

Source: "Public's Priorities for US Asylum Policy: More Judges for Cases, Safe Conditions for Migrants," Pew Research Center, August 12, 2019. www.people-press.org.

Despite the low rate of acceptance, since 2009 the number of asylum cases reviewed by immigration judges annually has risen dramatically. During most of the early 2000s, the USCIS conducted about five thousand credible fear screenings a year. But in 2009 the Obama administration implemented new asylum procedures. If migrants who were caught crossing the border illegally asked for asylum, they were detained and given a credible fear screening. If they passed this initial screening—and USCIS data indicates that nearly 90 percent of all asylum seekers passed from 2009 to 2016—they were released into the United States until their formal hearing before an immigration judge.

Consequently, there was a huge increase in asylum requests, mostly by migrants from El Salvador, Guatemala, and Honduras. These migrants—most of whom claimed to be fleeing from political instability or drug-related gang violence—learned that requesting asylum offered them the opportunity to live in the United States while their cases were considered. Beginning in 2009 many who illegally crossed the border did not even try to hide from the border patrol. Once they got across the border, they simply sat down and waited for agents to apprehend them so they could request asylum.

Funding for immigration courts and judges failed to keep pace with the increasing caseload, resulting in significant backlogs. In 2013 the USCIS conducted over 36,000 credible fear screenings, more than seven times as many as in 2009. In 2016 the number of credible fear screenings exceeded 94,000. And still people kept coming over the border. By August 2018 the USCIS had over 733,000 immigration cases pending, more than half of them involving asylum requests. The average wait time for an asylum hearing was 721 days. By September 2019 there were more than 1 million pending cases, and the average wait time for a hearing exceeded 800 days (2 years and 2+ months).

There are only about 425 immigration judges in the US asylum system, so this backlog of cases is daunting. It could be even worse, however. According to the DHS, approximately half of those who pass the credible fear screening and are released into the country never actually complete an asylum application, disappearing into the population instead. Immigration advocates have proposed that many of these migrants may have thought that the initial credible fear screening meant that they had received asylum and did not understand there were still more steps to the process. Others contend that many of these people have intentionally abused the system to live in the United States illegally. Then-attorney general Jeff Sessions commented on this abuse in 2017:

> We have a generous asylum policy that is meant to protect those who, through no fault of their own, cannot co-exist in their home country no matter where they go because of persecution based on fundamental things like their religion or nationality. Unfortunately, this system is currently subject to rampant abuse and fraud. And as this system becomes overloaded with fake claims, it cannot deal effectively with just claims. The surge in trials, hearings, appeals, [and] bond proceedings has been overwhelming.[22]

Trump's Response

During his 2016 presidential campaign, Donald Trump promised to end what he referred to as the "catch-and-release" asylum policies of the Obama administration. Just as with refugee policy, Trump began implementing changes soon after taking office. In January 2017 he announced that anyone caught crossing the border illegally—including those requesting asylum—would face criminal prosecution and prison terms of six months to two years. Illegal border crossers who sought asylum were detained in jail-like facilities along the border, rather than being released into the country to await a hearing.

In April 2018 the Trump administration began a highly controversial program of separating migrant families—adults were transferred into the prison system, while their children were placed into a program for children run by the Office of Refugee

"We have a generous asylum policy that is meant to protect those who, through no fault of their own, cannot co-exist in their home country no matter where they go because of persecution based on fundamental things like their religion or nationality."[22]

—Jeff Sessions, former US attorney general

Resettlement. Because of shortages in funding and bed space, to accommodate the children the government had to erect tent cities in the desert and temporarily house some migrant children on military bases.

The program was widely criticized. "What the administration has decided to do is to separate children from their parents to try to send a message that if you cross the border with children, your children are going to be ripped away from you," said Republican senator from Maine Susan Collins. "That's traumatizing to the children who are innocent victims, and it is contrary to our values in this country."[23] Under intense pressure, the policy was revoked after a few months.

Also in 2018, CBP officers began limiting the number of people who could request asylum each day. When asylum seekers arrived at a port of entry at the US-Mexico border, they were told they had to put their name on a waiting list, return to Mexico, and wait for their turn to request asylum. The administration defended this policy by arguing that it would enable immigration officials to process claims faster. But migrant camps in Mexico bloomed because officials were only able to process a small percentage of the thousands of new migrants who arrived at the border each week.

Along with these limits, in 2018 the DHS also implemented the Migrant Protection Protocols, a new set of rules requiring those who applied for asylum to return to Mexico and wait for their claims to be processed, rather than waiting in the United States. This policy was defended as necessary and criticized as cruel. Either way one looks at it, by September 2019 there were at least twenty thousand migrants waiting in Mexico for their cases to be processed.

"What the administration has decided to do is to separate children from their parents to try to send a message that if you cross the border with children, your children are going to be ripped away from you. That's traumatizing to the children who are innocent victims, and it is contrary to our values in this country."[23]

—US senator Susan Collins

Unaccompanied Children

A controversial aspect of the current migrant crisis involves the large number of children who have arrived at the US-Mexico border without parents. Until recently, unaccompanied migrant children rarely tried to enter the United States. However, since 2014 more than 250,000 unaccompanied children have requested asylum. This influx has strained existing programs intended to help young refugees.

The CBP can detain unaccompanied children at the border for up to twenty days. At this point, the Office of Refugee Resettlement takes custody of the children. This government agency is responsible for finding family members or other sponsors in the United States who can care for the children. If no sponsors are found, a licensed care facility takes care of the children until they are adults.

Due to the increased number of asylum cases and the shortage of resources for immigration issues, it can be a challenge for the CBP and Office of Refugee Resettlement to completely vet sponsors in the twenty-day period. Consequently, human traffickers have taken advantage of loopholes in the system. In one 2016 case, six teenage Guatemalan girls caught at the US border were released into the custody of Ana Angelica Pedro-Juan, who claimed to be a relative. Authorities later discovered that she had conspired with a trafficker named Aroldo Castillo-Serrano, who had smuggled the girls to the border to use them as forced labor on an egg farm in Ohio.

Changing Policy

In July 2019 the US Department of Justice and the DHS jointly issued a new rule that radically changes the asylum process. Under this new rule, most migrants would not be eligible for asylum in the United States unless they had previously applied for protection in the first "safe" country they passed through on the way to the US border. This means that migrants from Central America must first request asylum in Mexico before coming to the United States. The Trump administration has explained the rule change as an effort to manage the backlog of asylum cases but also to identify migrants who genuinely fear persecution as opposed to those who are merely seeking economic opportunity. "This rule mitigates the strain on the country's immigration system by more efficiently identifying aliens who are misusing the asylum system to enter and remain in the United States rather than legitimately seeking urgent protection from persecution or torture,"[24] notes the official rule as published in the *Federal Register*.

Civil liberties organizations immediately filed a federal lawsuit challenging the new rules. "This is the latest—and deeply dangerous—effort by the Trump administration to inflict maximal cruelty on vulnerable people fleeing desperate conditions for safety here,"[25] said Baher Azmy, legal director of the Center for Constitutional Rights. Federal courts initially blocked the program, but on September 11, 2019, the US Supreme Court ruled that the policy could be implemented while the lawsuit worked its way through the lower courts.

Separated from their parents, children sit behind fencing at an immigrant detention center in McAllen, Texas. In April 2018, the Trump administration began the highly controversial program of separating migrant families.

No Easy Solution

Most experts agree that new rules and procedures will not stop people from migrating north to seek better opportunities in the United States. From 2014 to 2018, approximately half a million people were caught crossing the US border illegally. In 2019, despite the Trump administration's more restrictive policies, the number of illegal border crossers jumped to about 1 million.

Many people believe that those who are barred from entering the country legally will keep looking for other ways in, risking their lives in the process. Writes David Frum in the *Atlantic*:

> Virtually none of those trying to cross the Rio Grande are fleeing state-sponsored persecution, although many do face real hardship at home. Many are people living in a globalized world willing to brave big risks with their lives and money in hope of bettering their situation. Almost all of us in the United States are descended from people like that, so of course we sympathize. But the policies that made sense for the United States in 1890 do not make sense in 2020.[26]

Chapter Five

Redefining Refugees

In September 2019 Hurricane Dorian hit the Bahamas with devastating effect. The Category 5 hurricane—one of the most powerful Atlantic hurricanes ever recorded—stalled over the northernmost islands of the archipelago for two days. Two of the largest islands, Grand Bahama and Great Abaco, were pounded with heavy rain, waves up to 25 feet (7.6 m) high, and powerful winds up to 220 miles per hour (354 kph). By the time the deadly storm passed, dozens had been killed and roughly half the homes on the islands destroyed, leaving over seventy thousand people homeless. Those who survived Dorian had to cope with shortages of food and potable water. Roads and other infrastructure were so badly damaged that for several weeks the Bahamian government was unable to restore power and sanitation systems, reopen health care clinics, or provide many other essential services to islanders.

The United States and other countries immediately offered help, providing food and water, temporary shelter, portable stoves, and other forms of emergency assistance. Even with that help, tens of thousands of Bahamians began leaving the devastated islands. Many traveled to Florida, hoping to stay with friends or relatives in the United States during the months (and possibly years) that it will take to rebuild their home communities. Under a long-standing US immigration policy, certain residents of the Bahamas who hold a valid passport can legally visit the United States without a tourist visa, so long as they pass through a CBP preclearance center in either Nassau or Freeport, the Bahamas's two major cities. Dozens of state and federal legislators asked the Trump administration to temporarily waive the visa requirements to allow additional Bahamians into the country. However, the DHS refused to relax its visa requirements, although it did continue processing visa applications.

Another issue involved how long these Bahamian visitors could stay in the United States. Nonimmigrant visas often expire within six months, meaning that the refugees would have to return to the island unless they received permission to remain in the United States beyond that term. But policy makers in Washington, DC, soon signaled that such an extension was unlikely. In

In September 2019, Hurricane Dorian hit the Bahamas with devastating effect. Tens of thousands of Bahamians have since left the islands to seek temporary refuge in the United States.

mid-September news outlets reported that the Trump administration would not make Bahamians eligible for a refugee program known as Temporary Protected Status (TPS).

The TPS Program

TPS is a special asylum program created by the Immigration Act of 1990. Under this program, the DHS may designate a country for TPS because of a civil war or other ongoing armed conflict; because of a natural disaster, such as a hurricane or earthquake;

Climate Refugees

A new category of refugees is forming. These are people who are forced to leave their homes due to sudden or long-term changes to their local environment. They are known as climate refugees.

Kiribati is a group of islands in the Pacific Ocean that is home to about one hundred thousand people. The islands are, on average, just 6 feet (1.8 m) above sea level, and many experts predict that by 2100 they will be underwater due to rising ocean levels. Flooding has already begun in some low-lying areas, including the village where Ioane Teitiota lived. He and his wife left Kiribati in 2007 and settled illegally in New Zealand. Facing deportation in 2010, Teitiota requested asylum, claiming refugee status due to the effects of climate change on Kiribati. His request was denied, so he appealed through the New Zealand courts.

Finally, in July 2015 the Supreme Court of New Zealand denied his asylum request. The court confirmed earlier decisions that Teitiota did not face "serious harm," adding, "there is no evidence that the Government of Kiribati is failing to take steps to protect its citizens from the effects of environmental degradation to the extent that it can." The ruling also noted that Teitiota had the option to live in areas of Kiribati not yet subject to regular flooding. Since then, courts in other countries have concurred in this decision that climate refugees are not entitled to the same protection as refugees from conflict or persecution.

Teitiota v Chief Executive of the Ministry of Business, Innovation and Employment, NZSC 107, July 20, 2015. www.courtsofnz.govt.nz.

or because of some other dire but temporary situation, such as a disease epidemic. Once a TPS designation is made, individuals from the country in question who are in the United States may apply for asylum. Upon approval, they receive the right to live and work in the United States without fear of deportation until their country's TPS designation is removed. The initial TPS protection lasts for eighteen months but can be renewed so long as the unsafe conditions in the home country continue to exist. TPS does not make a person eligible for permanent residency or change his or her immigration status in any other way.

Today there are approximately 318,000 asylees living in the United States under TPS protection. Among those who were driven to the United States by natural disasters are Haitians, who were admitted after a devastating earthquake caused widespread destruction in 2010. The largest group of TPS asylees is from El Salvador; they were admitted in response to a powerful earthquake in January 2001. Thousands from Honduras and Nicaragua were admitted in the wake of Hurricane Mitch, the deadliest Atlantic hurricane ever recorded, which hit Central America in the fall of 1998. "Generally, under circumstances like this really catastrophic hurricane . . . TPS would be granted," Doris Meissner, an expert with the Migration Policy Institute, said in reference to Hurricane Dorian. "But at the same time, [the Trump] administration has made it very clear that it thinks that TPS has been overused."[27]

At the time Barack Obama left office in early 2017, people from thirteen countries were eligible for TPS status. In addition to El Salvador, Haiti, Honduras, and Nicaragua, these included Guinea, Liberia, Nepal, Sierra Leone, Somalia, Sudan, South Sudan, Syria, and Yemen. However, the incoming Trump administration soon targeted TPS as part of its effort to reduce immigration and deport foreigners from the United States. First the government ended TPS protection for citizens of Guinea, Liberia, and Sierra Leone in May 2017. Immigrants from those West African countries had been protected since 2014 due to

A medical team in Liberia buries a person suspected of having died from Ebola. The 2014 outbreak of the deadly virus in West Africa sent many people fleeing to the United States for refuge.

an outbreak of the highly contagious and deadly disease Ebola. The DHS determined that the epidemic had ended, so there was no reason citizens could not return home safely. Next, between January and June 2018, the DHS announced that it would terminate TPS status for El Salvador, Haiti, Honduras, Nepal, Nicaragua, and Sudan after a twelve-to-eighteen-month transition period. However, lawsuits filed against the DHS have delayed the termination of TPS status for residents of these countries until a final court decision on the cases.

A New Kind of Refugee

This phasing out of TPS is in line with the Trump administration's overall policies toward refugees, asylum seekers, and immigrants. At every turn, the administration has tried to restrict foreigners from resettling in the United States. However, many experts agree that Trump's approach will not work in the long term because it ignores several important factors. One is population growth: the world population grew from 2.5 billion in 1950 to around 7.7 billion in 2020 and is expected to surpass 10 billion in 2055. Most of the growth will occur in the developing world, particularly Africa and Latin America—the two regions where a majority of refugees and asylees seeking entrance to the United States come from today. As growing populations strain the resources of these regions, the number of migrants seeking refuge in America will only grow larger.

The pressure of population growth will be compounded by other problems, particularly climate change, which will drive new waves of migration to wealthier nations like the United States. According to a 2014 report by the International Organization for Migration, at least 25 million people—and possibly 1 billion people—will be forced to relocate due to the effects of climate change by 2100. Rising sea levels already threaten low-lying island nations like Kiribati, the Maldives, and Tuvalu. Many scientists agree that rising temperatures contribute to increased wildfires, longer droughts, and more powerful storms like Hurricane Dorian.

Research supports the claim that climate change will increase the number of asylum seekers. A 2018 study published in the journal *Science* concluded that asylum applications to the European Union could increase by 28 percent, to nearly 450,000 per year, by the end of the century due to climate change. "Our findings support the assessment that climate change, especially continued warming, will add another 'threat multiplier' that induces people to seek refuge abroad," write researchers Anouch Missirian and Wolfram Schlenker. "Weather impacts in low-income source countries will not be confined to those countries or regions but will instead likely spill over into developed countries through increased refugee flows."[28]

> "Climate change, especially continued warming, will add another 'threat multiplier' that induces people to seek refuge abroad."[28]
>
> —Anouch Missirian and Wolfram Schlenker, environmental researchers

People who are forced to leave their homes due to sudden or long-term changes to their local environment are called "climate refugees." Like other refugees, they leave areas that are no longer safe. However, climate refugees are not guaranteed protection under the UN's Convention Relating to the Status of Refugees and Protocol Relating to the Status of Refugees. "Technically, in the context of legal and political systems, climate refugees don't exist," writes science journalist Maggie Koerth-Baker. "There's no space for them in international law and no special plans for how to treat them in the United States when they arrive. Here and around the world, fleeing climate change means running to bureaucracies as inhospitable to your survival as the places you left behind."[29]

> "Technically, in the context of legal and political systems, climate refugees don't exist. There's no space for them in international law and no special plans for how to treat them in the United States when they arrive."[29]
>
> —Maggie Koerth-Baker, science journalist

Addressing the Problem

Many countries have acknowledged the shortcomings of the current system and have been considering new ways to help refugees, migrants, and displaced people. In 2007 the UN launched the Global Forum on Migration and Development so that governments could begin discussing opportunities and challenges related to migration. As a result of these talks, in 2013 the forum helped produce an eight-point agenda for international action on migration, including a guarantee of rights and protections for all migrants, not just those designated as refugees under the UN convention.

In September 2016 the UN hosted a Summit for Refugees and Migrants in New York City, which was attended by representatives of 193 countries. The summit produced the New York Declaration for Refugees and Migrants, a statement in which UN member states agreed to begin working toward a new framework for addressing large movements of refugees and migrants, protecting their human rights regardless of status, and providing greater support for countries that rescue, receive, and host large numbers of refugees and migrants. Over the next two years, two separate intergovernmental discussion groups emerged: one dealing with migrants, the other with refugees. Both groups produced documents for consideration by the UN General Assembly in 2018.

The Global Compact for Safe, Orderly and Regular Migration, also known as the Marrakech Compact, was endorsed by the General Assembly on December 19, 2018. The compact states

Pressure to Leave Host Countries

While a small percentage of Syrian refugees are beginning to return home, for some refugees the decision to leave may not be entirely voluntary. The leaders of host countries have strongly encouraged Syrians to return, claiming that the country is safe now that the Bashar al-Assad regime has regained control. Many people in Lebanon, Jordan, and Turkey consider Syrian refugees to be a burden on their economies and a security threat to their societies. "Syrian refugees are often blamed for everything that goes wrong in Lebanon," writes journalist Tesbih Habbal. "Anti-refugee sentiment is perpetuated by Lebanese actors, journalists, and media. Lebanese leaders from across the political spectrum utilize anti-refugee rhetoric and look for ways to push Syrians to go back home."

The principle of non-refoulement prevents governments from forcing refugees to return to their country of origin until the danger has ended. But the Lebanese government has torn down refugee settlements, made it nearly impossible for refugees to find jobs, and forced some refugees to sign "voluntary" repatriation forms that enable the government to send them back to Syria. "Lebanese politicians justify their actions by claiming that Syrian refugees are no longer living in fear, and therefore there is no reason for them to stay in Lebanon," writes Habbal. "But despite Assad's claims of victory and politicians' narratives of stability and security, Syria today might not be any safer than it was before."

Tesbih Habbal, "Syrians in Lebanon: A Life of Misery, or a Return to the Unknown," *MENASource* (blog), Atlantic Council, July 8, 2019. www.atlanticcouncil.org.

that all migrants have human rights that are deserving of protection, regardless of their refugee status. It calls for countries to respect the rights of migrants who cross their borders by not detaining the migrants for long periods in unsafe conditions, by offering them medical care and other basic services when needed, and by helping those who are permitted to remain in the country to integrate economically and socially. It also says that the countries where migrants come from must play a constructive role in preventing illegal immigration and bringing back those caught crossing borders without proper documentation.

Importantly, the Marrakech Compact was among the first official agreements to acknowledge that climate change helps drive international migration. One goal stated in the compact is to "identify, develop and strengthen solutions for migrants compelled to leave their countries of origin owing to slow-onset natural disasters, the adverse effects of climate change, and environmental degradation, such as desertification, land degradation, drought and sea level rise."[30] Several sections of the compact refer to the need for new policies that can help climate refugees.

Limited Effectiveness

The Marrakech Compact will not result in immediate changes in the ways that economic migrants and climate refugees are treated. While the compact addresses migrant rights, it explicitly reinforces the current legal difference between migrants and refugees. The compact also does nothing to actually resolve the problems of wide-scale migration but simply identifies a variety of potential areas for continuing discussion. Finally, the Marrakech Compact is nonbinding, meaning that countries cannot be forced to change their immigration policies or accept economic migrants they do not want, and there are no sanctions for countries that do not adhere to the compact's commitments.

Although more than 150 countries have agreed to be part of the Marrakech Compact, more than forty of the UN's member

In 2018 Typhoon Mangkhut (pictured) wreaked destruction on several nations in the western Pacific. Many experts predict a rise in asylum seekers from countries impacted by the destructive effects of global climate change.

states—including the United States—have declined to sign the agreement. President Obama had been a vocal supporter of the 2016 summit that produced the New York Declaration for Refugees and Migrants, but after President Trump took office in 2017, the United States pulled out of the discussions. "Our decisions on immigration policies must always be made by Americans and Americans alone," declared Trump's ambassador to the UN, Nikki Haley. "We will decide how best to control our borders and who will be allowed to enter our country. The global approach in the New York Declaration is simply not compatible with US sovereignty."[31]

Major industrialized nations like Australia, Austria, the Czech Republic, Hungary, Israel, Italy, and Switzerland have also refused to endorse the Marrakech Compact. Like the United States, they have cited concern that the compact would interfere with their immigration policies and would increase the number of migrants worldwide, rather than controlling migrant flows. "We're not going to sign any document that's not in our national interest and it's not in our national interest to sign our border protection policy over to the UN,"[32] commented Australian interior minister Peter Dutton in July 2018.

> "Our decisions on immigration policies must always be made by Americans and Americans alone. We will decide how best to control our borders and who will be allowed to enter our country."[31]
>
> —Nikki Haley, US ambassador to the UN

What the Future Holds

Even as US government policies toward refugees and asylum seekers have hardened, the need for international engagement has grown. The crises that have led to rising numbers of refugees and asylum seekers—war and conflict, violence, poverty, persecution, and climate change—have not subsided. If the United States and other nations do not do more to help developing countries build democratic institutions and strong economies, desperate people will continue to seek safety and opportunity for themselves and their families in countries around the world. "The only real option for tackling the refugee crisis is to address the causes of people's displacement, including terrorism, hunger, disease, oppression, inadequate infrastructure, scarce vital resources, a lack of jobs and economic prospects, and falling standards of living,"[33] notes Nirj Deva, a member of the European Parliament. Whether the world will rise to this challenge or ignore it remains to be seen.

Introduction: Seeking a Safe Place

1. Quoted in Save the Children, "Stories of Syrian Refugees," 2019. www.savethechildren.org.
2. Quoted in Save the Children, "Stories of Syrian Refugees."
3. Quoted in Haley Sweetland Edwards, "The Stories of Migrants Risking Everything for a Better Life," *Time*, January 24, 2019. https://time.com.

Chapter One: Protecting the Victims of Conflict

4. Quoted in William D. Rubenstein, *The Myth of Rescue: Why the Democracies Could Not Have Saved More Jews from the Nazis*. New York: Routledge, 1997, p. 50.
5. Ishaan Tharoor, "Europe's Fear of Muslim Refugees Echoes Rhetoric of 1930s Anti-Semitism," *Washington Post*, September 2, 2015. www.washingtonpost.com.
6. United Nations High Commissioner for Refugees, "Convention and Protocol Relating to the Status of Refugees." www.unhcr.org.
7. Barack Obama, "Remarks at Leaders Summit on Refugees," White House, September 20, 2016. https://obamawhitehouse.archives.gov.

Chapter Two: The Dangerous Life of a Refugee

8. Quoted in Catherine Bellamy et al., "The Lives and Livelihoods of Syrian Refugees: A Study of Refugee Perspectives and Their Institutional Environment in Turkey and Jordan," Humanitarian Policy Group, February 2017, p. 25. www.odi.org.
9. Quoted in Bellamy et al., "The Lives and Livelihoods of Syrian Refugees."
10. Elizabeth Cullen Dunn, "The Failure of Refugee Camps," *Boston Review*, September 28, 2015. http://bostonreview.net.
11. William Swing, "Practical Considerations for Effective Resettlement," *Forced Migration Review*, February 2017, p. 4.

12. Quoted in Monica Campbell, "Settled but Unsettled: 4 Years On, a Syrian Refugee Family Still Torn by US Policy," Public Radio International, June 21, 2019. www.pri.org.

Chapter Three: Resettling Refugees in the United States

13. Quoted in Fox News, "Trump: Syria Refugees Could Be the 'Ultimate Trojan Horse,'" *Hannity*, November 18, 2015. www.foxnews.com.
14. V.V.B., "Why America Does Not Take In More Syrian Refugees," *Economist*, October 18, 2015. www.economist.com.
15. Michelle Ye Hee Lee, "The Viral Claim That 'Not One' Refugee Resettled Since 9/11 Has Been 'Arrested on Domestic Terrorism Charges,'" *Washington Post*, November 19, 2015. www.washingtonpost.com.
16. Donald J. Trump, "Executive Order Protecting the Nation from Foreign Terrorist Entry into the United States," White House, January 27, 2017. www.whitehouse.gov.
17. Quoted in Matt Zapotosky et al., "Revised Executive Order Bans Travelers from Six Muslim-Majority Countries from Getting New Visas," *Washington Post*, March 6, 2017. www.washingtonpost.com.
18. Quoted in International Rescue Committee, "A Year of Unwelcome: How the Trump Administration Has Sabotaged America's Welcome," November 21, 2017. www.rescue.org.
19. Quoted in Julie Hirschfeld Davis and Michael D. Shear, "Trump Administration Considers a Drastic Cut in Refugees Allowed to Enter US," *New York Times*, September 6, 2019. www.nytimes.com.

Chapter Four: A Broken Asylum System

20. Quoted in Nathan Gardels, "Refugees and Migrants Have Become a Blurred Challenge," *Washington Post*, December 20, 2018. https://beta.washingtonpost.com.
21. US Citizenship and Immigration Services, "Credible Fear FAQ," September 26, 2008. www.uscis.gov.
22. Quoted in US Department of Justice, "Attorney General Jeff Sessions Delivers Remarks to the Executive Office for Immigration Review," October 12, 2017. www.justice.gov.

23. Quoted in Billy Perrigo, "Here Are All the Republicans Who Criticized the Trump Administration's Family Separation Policy This Weekend," *Time*, June 18, 2018. https://time.com.
24. US Department of Justice and Executive Office for Immigration Review, "Asylum Eligibility and Procedural Modifications," *Federal Register*, July 16, 2019. www.federalregister.gov.
25. Quoted in American Civil Liberties Union, "Groups File Federal Lawsuit Challenging New Trump Asylum Restrictions," July 16, 2019. www.aclu.org.
26. David Frum, "America's Asylum System Is Profoundly Broken," *Atlantic*, July 3, 2019. www.theatlantic.com.

Chapter Five: Redefining Refugees

27. Quoted in Hannah Knowles, "Reports That US Won't Offer Bahamians 'Protected Status' While Islands Recover Don't Surprise Experts," *Washington Post*, September 11, 2019. www.washingtonpost.com.
28. Anouch Missirian and Wolfram Schlenker, "Asylum Applications Respond to Temperature Fluctuations," *Science*, December 22, 2017. https://science.sciencemag.org.
29. Maggie Koerth-Baker, "The World Isn't Ready for Climate Refugees," FiveThirtyEight, September 12, 2019. https://fivethirtyeight.com.
30. United Nations General Assembly, "Global Compact for Safe, Orderly and Regular Migration," December 11, 2018. https://undocs.org.
31. Quoted in US Mission to the United Nations, "United States Ends Participation in Global Compact on Migration," December 2, 2017. https://usun.usmission.gov.
32. Quoted in Amy Remeikis and Ben Doherty, "Dutton Says Australia Won't 'Surrender Our Sovereignty' by Signing UN Migration Deal," *Guardian* (Manchester), July 24, 2018. www.theguardian.com.
33. Nirj Deva, "Why There's Only One Real Solution to the Refugee Crisis," World Economic Forum, June 15, 2017. www.weforum.org.

Alight — www.wearealight.org

For more than forty years, this organization has helped refugees and displaced people survive conflict and crisis by providing humanitarian aid.

American Red Cross — www.redcross.org

The American Red Cross provides first aid, medical services, food and water, shelter, and other essential relief supplies to refugees and families displaced by conflict.

Amnesty International — www.amnesty.org

Amnesty International works to ensure justice and fair treatment for refugees and others who face discrimination throughout the world.

Migration Policy Institute — www.migrationpolicy.org

The Migration Policy Institute is an independent, nonpartisan think tank dedicated to analysis of the movement of people worldwide. The institute publishes books, reports, fact sheets, and the online journal *Migration Information Source*.

National Network for Immigrant and Refugee Rights — www.nnirr.org

The goal of the National Network for Immigrant and Refugee Rights is to promote a fair immigration and refugee policy in the United States and to defend and expand the rights of all immigrants and refugees, regardless of immigration status.

Refugee Council USA — http://rcusa.org

Refugee Council USA is a coalition of two dozen organizations that work to protect refugees and help them resettle in the United States.

Refugees International — www.refugeesinternational.org

Refugees International is an advocate group that attempts to bring issues of refugees, displacement, and human rights to the attention of policy makers and international organizations.

United Nations High Commissioner for Refugees (UNHCR) — www.unhcr.org

The UNHCR is a global organization dedicated to saving lives, protecting rights, and building a better future for refugees, forcibly displaced communities, and stateless people.

Books

Aviva Chomsky, *Undocumented: How Immigration Became Illegal*. Boston: Beacon, 2014.

Jim Gallagher, *Thinking Critically: Illegal Immigration*. San Diego: ReferencePoint, 2019.

Tom Gjelten, *A Nation of Nations: A Great American Immigration Story*. New York: Simon and Schuster, 2015.

Reece Jones, *Violent Borders: Refugees and the Right to Move*. New York: Verso, 2016.

Patrick Kingsley, *The New Odyssey: The Story of the Twenty-First-Century Refugee Crisis*. New York: Liveright, 2017.

John Moore, *Undocumented: Immigration and the Militarization of the United States–Mexico Border*. New York: Powerhouse, 2018.

Rick Schmerhorn, *Undocumented Immigrants and Homeland Security*. Philadelphia: Mason Crest, 2017.

Internet Sources

Elizabeth Cullen Dunn, "The Failure of Refugee Camps," *Boston Review*, September 28, 2015. http://bostonreview.net.

Haley Sweetland Edwards, "The Stories of Migrants Risking Everything for a Better Life," *Time*, January 24, 2019. https://time.com.

Laura King and Glen Johnson, "Death of Syrian Toddler Throws Global Spotlight onto Refugee Crisis," *Los Angeles Times*, September 3, 2015. www.latimes.com.

Maggie Koerth-Baker, "The World Isn't Ready for Climate Refugees," FiveThirtyEight, September 12, 2019. https://fivethirtyeight.com.

Andrea Pitzer, "Trump's 'Migrant Protection Protocols' Hurt the People They're Supposed to Help," *Washington Post*, July 18, 2019. www.washingtonpost.com.

Ishaan Tharoor, "Europe's Fear of Muslim Refugees Echoes Rhetoric of 1930s Anti-Semitism," *Washington Post*, September 2, 2015. www.washingtonpost.com.

About the Author

Jim Gallagher is the author of more than twenty books for young adults, including *Illegal Immigration* (ReferencePoint Press, 2019). His other books, written for various publishers, include *The Johnstown Flood*, *Causes of the Iraq War*, and *A Girl's/Guy's Guide to Conflict*. He lives in central New Jersey with his wife, LaNelle, and their three children.